The Key to
MOSCOW

THE KREMLIN

The Key to
MOSCOW

By HARRISON E. SALISBURY

Keys to the Cities Series

J. B. LIPPINCOTT COMPANY
Philadelphia and New York

The author wishes to thank the Embassy of the Union of Soviet
Socialist Republics in Washington for permission to use photographs on pages 6, 14, 29, 32, 42, 44, 45, 67, 102, 111, 112, 114, 120.
Also The Novosti Press Agency for those on pages 31, 115. All other
photographs are the author's.

KEYS TO THE CITIES SERIES

The Key to Boston *by George F. and Mildred Weston*
The Key to Chicago *by Martha Bennett King*
The Key to London *by Alicia Street*
The Key to Los Angeles *by W. W. Robinson*
The Key to Moscow *by Harrison E. Salisbury*
The Key to New York *by Alice Fleming*
The Key to Paris *by Marjory Stoneman Douglas*
The Key to Philadelphia *by Dorothy Loder*
The Key to Rome *by Monroe Stearns*
The Key to St. Louis *by Shirley Seifert*
The Key to San Francisco *by Charlotte Jackson*
The Key to Tokyo *by Walter J. Sheldon*
The Key to Vienna *by Raymond A. Wohlrabe and Werner E. Krusch*
The Key to Washington *by John Upton Terrell*

CONTENTS

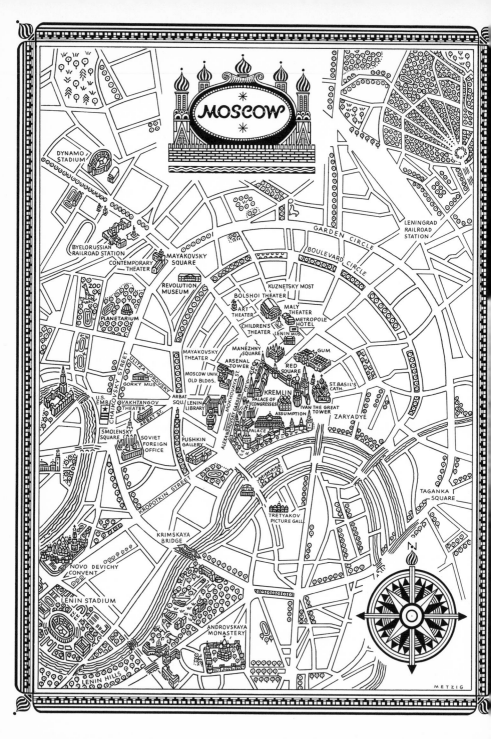

I. A Slow Train to Moscow

NOWADAYS most of us fly into Moscow. We board the big jet in London or Paris or Amsterdam and five or six hours later drop down from the substratosphere to land at the new chrome and glass Moscow airport, having caught no more than a glimpse of the Russian countryside, blurred and vague, forty thousand feet below. We zip into town by limousine, check in at a modern hotel, and half an hour later walk across Red Square and into the Kremlin, not quite sure which country we've landed in this time.

Far better to come to Moscow by train. Not the new daylight express from Leningrad, nor the antique Red Arrow, with its 1907 mahogany and brass International Sleeping Car. Instead, let's take the long way in from the West—Berlin, the Oder bridge at Frankfurt, the flat Polish plains, Warsaw, and Brest-Litovsk, the border town where war between Bolshevik Russia and the Kaiser's Germany ended in 1918. Then, on across the Pripet Marshes, desolate and poor, across the fields of Byelorussia, or White Russia, through Baranovichi, Minsk, Orsha, Smolensk, and Vyazma, finally into Moscow. It's an eighteen-hour trip from the Polish-Russian border. And more than two full days from Berlin.

Why take the long, slow, old route to Moscow? Why follow the route of Hitler's armies in 1941, of the Prussians in 1914, and Napoleon in 1812, the ancient path of invasion from the West? By coming this way we fix Moscow in space, in time, and in history. We approach the capital of "All the Russias" by crossing the very "Russias" themselves. We set a patient course across the steppe, the broad plain where earth and sky blend in the distance, where the forests stretch on and on and man is small in the Russian vastness. We come to Moscow not fresh from the bright paint of Amsterdam, the boulevards of Paris, or the gray stones of old London. We come over the endless distances of the Russian land and we have Russians for traveling companions rather than other tourists like ourselves.

Russian trains are long and wide (the rails are spaced six inches farther apart than ours) and slow. Rarely do they go more than thirty-five or forty miles an hour. They move stubbornly across the country, halting at the stations to load freight and board passengers. There's always time for travelers to stretch their legs, gossip with the peasant women selling roast chickens or dill pickles in twists of old newspaper. The Russians refill their tea kettles from the *kipyatok,* the boiling-water tap, replenish their thermos bottles, and inquire about the potato crop. Not until the warning bell do they scramble back aboard the train.

Train travel in Russia is leisurely, almost as leisurely as it was in the days of Tolstoy and Chekhov. It is comfortable, rather old-fashioned,

ACROSS THE STEPPES

and companionable. When Russians travel they relax, trade stories with their neighbors, and look out the windows at the passing forests of spruce, the swamps of tamarack, the wastes of scrub pine, the white birches, willowy as maidens, the fields of wheat or flax that flow from horizon to horizon, the peasant villages, with their log houses, wide dirt-and-grass streets, and tethered goats, the onion domes of the churches, the industrial cities, big, noisy, smoky, and always, somehow, half finished.

As we travel across Russia by train, our ears become accustomed to the rhythms of Russian speech. We get used to hearing *da* and *nyet.* There's a youngster with a *bayan,* a Russian accordion, in the car. He serenades the passengers with mournful Russian songs, sad melodies of unrequited love and lost gypsy sweethearts. Neighbors share their heavy black bread, their long garlicky sausage, and pickled ripe tomatoes. The fussy woman porter, or *provodnitza,* keeps a samovar bubbling at the end of the car. She serves tea, hot and fragrant, in thin glasses with metal glass holders. An old man with worn boots and a black suitcase bound with rope tells a story about Russia in the days of his youth, long before the Revolution, when landowners ruled the country. A couple of college boys make gentle fun of the old man. *"Dedushka,"* they say. "Grandpa, every-thing's changed now. Now, we are building a new Soviet society." The old man sighs. *"Da,"* he says. *"Da.* Yes. Everything is changing. But it's still Russia all the same."

Even the Russian alphabet begins to lose its mysteries. The curious P's, backward R's, re-versed N's, missplaced H's, and overgrown punc-tuation marks *do* mean something. It turns out that *Mockba* is nothing more than *Moskva.* And *Moskva,* of course, is Moscow. *Россія* is *Rossiya.* Russia! *Меню, бифштекс, суп* suddenly dissolve into menu, beefsteak, and soup.

There's a Russian who speaks enough English to explain the tale of the strange alphabet. How it was invented by a Greek missionary, Cyril, in the ninth century. How Cyril brought the gospel to the untutored Slavic tribes then settled in Bul-garia. The Slavs had no alphabet of their own. So he made one up, using Greek letters and in-venting new ones for sounds that existed in the Slav tongue but not in Greek.

Aboard the western *kuriersky,* or express, we begin to get some of the feel of Russia, of what Moscow means to the Russians—why it is the mecca of the gray and dusty steppe, the magnet of peasant eyes, the goal of young Russian dreams. We sense its firm and solid roots in the

PAINTED TOWERS AND SPARKLING DOMES

sour-smelling Russian soil. We understand Gorky when he writes that "as far as the eye can see stretches an endless plain, and in the midst of it stands an insignificant wretched little man, cast away upon this dreary earth to labor like a galley slave." Moscow begins to loom ahead, not as the dowdy cousin of streamlined New York, but as the wonder city of generations of "dark people," born to the *izba,* or peasant hut, the kerosene lamp, and the village well, with its rope and wooden bucket.

For centuries, travelers coming across the steppe-and-forest have been amazed at their first sight of Moscow. A French visitor wrote nearly a hundred fifty years ago: "In the midst of this solitude suddenly I saw spring up thousands of painted towers and sparkling domes. This was the city."

Those were the days of the most autocratic of Russian Czars, Nicholas I; of Russian barons so rich they could ride for days without crossing the boundaries of their estates; of serfdom, in which Russian peasants were held in virtual slavery; of diamond-bedecked princesses, swathed in sables, and ermine; of palaces and grand balls; of idealistic young reformers and fanatic anarchists who wanted to bomb this world out of existence; of the horse-drawn troikas with three spirited chargers and black and silver harness; of Moscow's traditional "forty times forty" churches, whose peals of bells rolled like musical thunder over the city.

Today the Czars and the serfs, the riches, the ermine, and the troikas, the young reformers, the anarchists, and many of the churches are gone. Moscow is a Communist city, the capital of the Soviet state. It is run by the Presidium of the Communist Party and all the land and industry have long since been turned over to the government. But Moscow still rises up from the central Russian plain like a vision to surprise all who approach it. The first surprise is the city's size, the way it sprawls across the rolling countryside. As far back as the time of the American Revolution, Moscow covered more ground than any other city in Europe. Today it is second only to London and expanding rapidly, bulldozers furiously chewing away on the outskirts as the authorities try to catch up with forty years of pent-up demand for housing—few places for people to live in had been built during the first four decades of the Revolution.

No longer do the onion domes and bell towers of the churches loom over the forests that still form a green belt that laps at the edge of the city. Now, no matter from what direction we ap-

THE "TALL BUILDINGS" OF MODERN MOSCOW

proach, our first distant sight is of the sparkling turrets of the eight "tall buildings" which Generalissimo Joseph Stalin, Communist ruler of Russia from 1924 to 1953, ordered built just before he died. Moscow began by calling these buildings skyscrapers—they are fifteen to thirty-two stories high. But Stalin put a stop to that. He thought that the word "skyscraper" smacked too much of New York. So they are "tall buildings" to this day.

Whatever else he left behind (and it will be long before Stalin's terror fades from memory), the turrets of his tall buildings have permanently changed Moscow. In New York's fabulous canyons Stalin's towers would soon be lost, but in horizontal Moscow they give the city style and perspective.

For better or for worse Moscow will always bear the stamp of Stalin, just as it bears the stamp of the other powerful rulers of the past— Ivan the Great, Ivan the Terrible, Peter the Great, Catherine II, and Nicholas I. Each one made an indelible contribution to the great capital of the Slav state. Moscow has changed enormously in the nearly fifty years since the Communists came to power. It is a modern, vibrant city. Its streets are paved. Its factories hum to the tempo of the latest technology. But, nevertheless, the Moscow of today, like the Russia of today, is a mosaic in which all the elements of the past are mixed with those of the present like the colors of a painter's palette.

AN ELEMENT OF THE PAST

OLD MOSCOW AND NEW

II. THE "WHITE STONE" CITY

OLD MOSCOW was crowded, low, and dirty. More than one traveler recorded his disappointment. The view from afar of dazzling colors and bizarre domes faded when you got close. The paint was flaking off. Most of the buildings were wooden. The Russians called Moscow the "White Stone" city, but the stone was not very white and, aside from the Kremlin, the city walls, and a few churches, it was still a wooden town. The streets were seas of mud across which pedestrians moved on rickety wooden bridges. The city had no plan and few sewers. Cattle and goats grazed in open fields. It was more like a collection of villages than a city. The houses didn't face the streets. And the streets followed no pattern. Some were narrow as alleys. Others were two hundred yards wide—as wide as the village pastures in the Ukraine. Most people still lived in log *izbas*, the

SOME STREETS STILL ARE MUDDY

peasant huts, just as in the country. Many of the
poor lived in "black" izbas—huts with no chim-
neys, just a hole in the roof or a wooden stack to
let out the smoke.

A traveler in 1561 reported, "Moscow is
wooden, not stone. A street may end and then
start again, across a field." Fifty years later an
Italian wrote that "Moscow has very wide streets
on which four carts can move abreast. When it
rains there is so much mud no one can venture
forth without boots." And a German observed in
1673 that Moscow's "streets are paved not with

stone but with wooden planks which are always swimming in mud."

In the seventeenth and eighteenth centuries when a landowner came to Moscow he brought his serfs with him, sometimes by the hundreds. They settled—cattle, pigs, chickens, and all—in a collection of log huts. In the center was a big courtyard where the "master" lived. In those times the population of Moscow was ordinarily counted by the number of "courtyards" rather than the number of houses or residents. There were sixteen thousand courtyards in 1701. In 1939 a count was taken again and there were still thirty thousand courtyards in the city.

At first it seems today as though old Moscow has vanished. You catch no glimpse of it around the Byelorussian railroad station, where the train from the west comes in. If you drive in from the Sheremetovo International Airport you speed along a six-lane highway, equipped with clover-leaves, overpasses, underpasses, neon lighting— all the trappings of the automobile age. True, there are wooden peasant huts in the suburban outskirts of Moscow, built of logs, just as they were three hundred years ago. Here and there you may see a *telega,* or peasant wagon, and a horse with a strange Russian yoke, a big clumsy affair made of wood. There are many more trucks than cars on the highway and the gasoline (or benzine, as they call it) has an acrid odor new to our noses.

But soon the countryside gives way to octagonal blocks of new apartment buildings, some finished and some surrounded by big cranes and scrambling work crews.

Inside the city there are boulevards and trees; pleasant-looking buildings; squares with fountains and squares with statues; more and more cars. Militiamen (as they call Russian policemen) direct a complex system of traffic lights from little glass-enclosed stalls at the main intersections. By the time we arrive at the hotel in the heart of the city, we have seen big new apartment houses, wide new boulevards, fine new store fronts, traffic jams and smartly uniformed policemen, crowds of people and Soviet automobiles that look like

WOODEN PEASANT HUTS

our own models of three or four years ago. Where is the old Moscow? Has it vanished entirely?

Not at all. In fact, it's just around the corner from the hotel! Just through that handsome pair of iron gates that leads from the new red stone building on Gorky Street. Duck past the archway a score of steps and there it is—the old Moscow of the history books. A little white-painted church with a deep blue onion dome spattered with golden stars. An old *babushka,* a grandmother with a black shawl over her head and shoulders, kissing an ikon on the wall beside the street, and crossing herself as she does. A hundred pigeons clustered around a bird-feeding station. Youngsters skipping rope in the cluttered courtyard, the girls in school uniforms of brown jumpers and white aprons, the boys with visored school caps and red kerchiefs. There's a bread store across the street with a red-cheeked, white-aproned, blond-haired girl in charge, and the yeasty smell of the warm brown loaves brings water to the mouth.

Here the buildings are not all new and shining. One is an old house from which most of the plaster that covers its log construction has cracked away. Another is an apartment house of reddish brick that looks as if it had been standing for sixty years, but a bearded old man sitting outside on a wooden bench says that it was put up only a short while ago. The court-yard where the youngsters are playing is bordered on three sides with buildings. Parts of it are covered with broken pavement. In one corner there are some sunflowers growing, and in the center there is what appears to be the remains of an old well.

This is a scene typical of Moscow. The blend of the new and the old, the new that looks al-ready old, the unfamiliar and the familiar, the East and the West, the Russian and the Euro-pean.

"Moskva, Moskva, lubimy gorod," sighs the old man. "Moscow, Moscow, beloved city," chant the youngsters as they skip rope. "Moscow, Mos-cow, our dear Moscow," recites the tallow-haired young poet to the girl with whom he sits on the park bench.

Beloved city . . . dear city . . . hated city . . . feared city . . . All of these Moscow has been in the 815 years of her recorded history. She has been ruled by men called Great, and by others called Terrible. But she has never had a Czar named the Good, or a commissar called the Kind.

No one knows just how long Moscow has

stood on the banks of the big curve of the Moskva River. There was probably a settlement on the forested hill where the Kremlin now rises for many years before the first mention in an old chronicle—an entry that is dated 1147 and tells, prophetically, of murder, duplicity, and aggression.

Moscow is a young city as Europe measures time. London is more than twice as old and so is Paris. Even in Russia Moscow is a latecomer. The history of Kiev, Russia's ancient capital, for instance, goes back nearly three thousand years.

Today Moscow is a great capital with more than five million population—the biggest city in Russia, the biggest industrial city of the Soviet Union, the bustling center of the whole Communist world. Every day a million visitors flood the wide Moscow streets. Missions from India, dark and colorful in turbans and saris; new African prime ministers; students from Paris, New York, and Burma; businessmen from Hamburg and tourists from Los Angeles pour in and out of the big new hotels. Crowds turn out at the airports to welcome a basketball team from the United States, a dancing troupe from Egypt, or the Prince and Princess of Cambodia.

Less than a hundred years ago Moscow was a provincial, sleepy "bear's corner," rusticating

quietly in the backwash of imperial St. Petersburg, the city at the mouth of the Neva River built by Peter the Great as his "window into Europe." St. Petersburg was Russia's capital from 1712 onwards. Two centuries passed before Lenin transferred the capital back to Moscow in 1918 as a "temporary" measure. He was afraid that the Germans might seize Petrograd (St. Petersburg was renamed Petrograd in World War I. It is now known as Leningrad). Long since, the "temporary" measure has become permanent.

Sometimes Moscow seems like the strangest, most foreign city in the world—a maze of signs in queer Cyrillic letters, a clatter of language that sounds like gibberish, a mixture of peoples from the far ends of the earth. Some have high

... FROM ALL PARTS OF RUSSIA

Mongol cheekbones. Others have slanting Oriental eyes. There are many with broad Slavic foreheads. Some men shave their heads like billiard balls. And others wear beards that reach to their waists. It's no surprise to learn that some 185 different nationalities—Great Russians, Little Russians, Ukrainians, Georgians, Armenians, Tadjiks, Uzbeks, Kirghiz, Eskimos, and many more—live in the Soviet Union. Not that all the people look so different. There are youngsters who would get lost in any American crowd, youngsters with snub noses and freckled faces, blue eyes and grinning mouths. There are girls with straight, pale-blond hair done in long pigtails, tied with white, red, or blue ribbons. And others with long golden braids twisted around their heads like crowns.

But what is surprising is to see women in cotton-padded work jackets or coveralls setting bricks in the new buildings; running the big iron rollers that smooth the fresh asphalt paving; sweeping the streets with long witches' brooms of twigs; laying the storm sewers or loading heavy trucks.

Women do a lot more physical labor in Moscow than in Western cities. In part it is peasant tradition. They've always put their sturdy backs and strong arms into the chores of the farm. In part it is the Soviet system, the "equality of men and women" so far as work goes, as the Com-

WOMEN DO PHYSICAL LABOR

munists like to say. Or, as foreigners frequently rejoin, the equal right of men and women to dig ditches.

One thing the Communists haven't been able to change in Moscow is the weather. We think of Russia as the land of ice and snow, of cold winters, of travelers dashing across the blizzard-swept steppe, followed by wolf packs in full bay. The Moscow winter is cold and, in testimony of that, we notice that in every home, hotel, or public building there are permanent double windows. In winter the Moscow housewife seals up the windows to keep out the north wind. She pastes long strips of paper along the edges and in the space between the double-windows she puts cotton batting "to absorb the cold." Each window has one small hinged pane that can be opened in any weather. This is called a *fortichka*. In winter this serves many Russian families as a natural icebox. Butter and eggs and the meat for tomorrow's dinner are tucked between the two windows by opening the *fortichka*.

Actually, most of us have a slightly exaggerated idea of the terrible Russian winter. In Siberia, it is true, the temperature falls to fifty or even sixty degrees below zero. But in Moscow the climate is much like that of northern New England or Minnesota. Most of the time the thermometer stands between ten and twenty degrees above. Occasionally it drops to twenty or thirty below, but rarely lower. Lots of snow makes for good cross-country skiing. Even kindergarten children spend a good deal of time on skis.

The worst thing about Moscow's winter is that it is long and dark and gloomy. It begins in mid-October and does not end until mid-April. Moscow is so far north that in December and January the sun doesn't rise until about nine o'clock and it sets at two-thirty or a little after. No wonder the Russian peasants in winter traditionally pulled themselves up on top of their great Dutch-oven stoves and hibernated until the snow began to melt. There wasn't much incentive to do anything else. Some people blame the dark Russian winter for the gloomy Russian character we find in novels like *Crime and Punishment* or *The Brothers Karamazov*.

But if Moscow is a city of snow and cold in the winter, the summers make up for it. They are hot and bright with sunshine. When spring comes everyone sheds his heavy fur-lined coat and *valenki,* or felt boots. The people throng out into the street to let the warm sun touch their pale faces.

Every city has its style. New Yorkers stroll

GORKY STREET

down Fifth Avenue. Londoners dally in Hyde Park. In Paris young couples wander along the river Seine.

Moscow's Fifth Avenue is Gorky Street, a broad avenue of shops and hotels. Sometimes there are queues outside the shoe stores, the women's shops, or the fish markets. Shortages of goods and food have not vanished from the Moscow scene.

The parks in Moscow are seldom empty. Housing is crowded. People like to get out in the open for a little air. Even on frosty winter days they sit in warm coats and fur hats on the park benches with the temperature hovering around zero.

On summer nights strollers wander along the concrete abutments of the Moskva River or crowd aboard the restaurant boats tied up at the *naberzhnaya,* or embankment. Excursion boats go by with a swish of waves, a flash of lights, and the sound of a brassy band.

Best of all the Muscovites like to stroll into the great squares that lie in the heart of the city. One of these is Theater Square, with its Bolshoi Theater, the Metropolitan Opera House of Moscow; the Maly, or Little, Theater; the Children's Theater; and the famous Metropole Hotel. Another is Manezhny Square, which faces the Kremlin itself. And most famous, of course, is Red Square. Its name, in Russian, is not really Red Square at all. It is Krasnaya Ploshchad, which, literally translated, means Beautiful Place. The name, as Russians are quick to point out, goes back three hundred years. It has nothing to do with the Bolsheviks or the present-day "Reds." The words "beautiful" and "red" were one and the same in ancient Russian, because to the old

Russians no color was more beautiful than red.

Ever since there was a Moscow, people have been strolling about Red Square. They still do, pausing now and then to feed the pigeons, watch the changing of the guard at Lenin's Mausoleum, and listen to the great chimes of the Kremlin's Spassky Tower toll out the hours, the half-hours, and the quarter-hours.

This great plaza—1300 feet long and 520 feet wide—is one of the most vast of any capital in the world. It is big enough to accommodate four football fields. As many as two million people can—and have congregated here.

THE SPASSKY TOWER

If Moscow is the heart of Russia, Red Square and the Kremlin are the heart of the heart. They form the very nucleus of the nation which has evolved through the centuries from the Slavic tribes that early in the Christian epoch began to take root in the lands between the Carpathians and the low Urals. The tap of heels on the stone pavement, the tramp of marching boots, the high whine of cars whisking out of the Spassky Gate, the rumble of trucks, the spiel of the guides, the chatter of the sight-seers, the slow, muffled slap of the peasant *valenki,* the chiming of the hours from the Spassky Tower—these are the sounds of Red Square, the pulse beats of Russia's heart.

A CELBRATION IN RED SQUARE

THE KREMLIN FROM ACROSS THE MOSCOW RIVER

III. "There's Nothing Above the Kremlin"

"There's nothing above Moscow except the Kremlin and nothing above the Kremlin except heaven." So the peasants have said, generation after generation, regardless of whether the rulers in the Kremlin were Czars or false Czars, commissars or Communists, benevolent tyrants or cruel dictators.

Most of us think of the Kremlin as a building or a palace. We think of it as a grim, forbidding pile, a dungeon, a prison, a stronghold of Communism and conspiracy. For years it was a synonym for Stalin, a symbol of darkness and danger, another word for Evil.

All that the Kremlin has been. Some of it the Kremlin still is. But it is more, too. Much more. It is not just a building. It is a city within a city, and what a city! It is all the castles in our fairy tales, piled one upon the other. Nowhere else are there battlements so strange and crenelated, towers and redoubts, revetments and portculises, barbicans and lucarns in such profusion. It is King Arthur come to life in the midst of *The Arabian Nights*. It is Hans Christian Andersen mixed with the Caliph of Bagdad and Ivan Skivitzky Skavar.

Théophile Gautier, the French writer, called the Kremlin "the Acropolis, the holy spot, the Palladium and the very heart of Russia!" His fellow countryman, the famous Marquis de Custine, described it as "The Mont Blanc of fortresses, a barbarian Pantheon, the Alcazar of the Slavs."

What is this place of mysterious and sinister phrases, the Kremlin? It is an area roughly triangular, situated on the Borovitsky Hill, 125 feet above the Moskva River at the point where the small Neglinnaya River flows into it. Around the mile-and-a-half perimeter of the Kremlin runs a sixty-five-foot wall, studded by redoubts and towers—nineteen of all sizes and shapes— with three main gates, or entrances. Inside there is a jumble of churches, palaces, and ancient monuments, museums, theaters, office buildings and barracks, an armory, one of the newest and most modern assembly halls in Europe, the world's biggest cannon (which never was fired), the world's biggest bell (which never rang), state treasures worth the ransoms of a score of Czars, the seat of the Soviet Government, living quarters, restaurants, and repair shops. Underneath all this lies a maze of subterranean passages and tunnels so complicated, so old and vast that not even the police have been able to find them all or figure out where they run to. In a secret vault somewhere under the Kremlin, Ivan the Great hid away one of the world's great libraries. He sealed it up nearly four hundred years ago.

THE ASSUMPTION
CATHEDRAL

Among the rare books, it is believed, was a copy of the manuscript of Homer's *Odyssey*. Years have been spent hunting this treasure trove, but it has never been found. Peter the Great spent thousands of rubles trying to locate it. One of his agents found a passageway that led across the Kremlin, underground, from the Moskva River to the Arsenal Tower. He discovered a blocked passage where he thought the library might be hidden, but he died before he could tunnel into the crypt. Later searchers have never been able to locate this spot. Czar Nicholas I and, in more recent times, Soviet rulers have sought the mysterious cache, but every effort has failed.

The outer walls of the Kremlin are twelve to eighteen feet thick. In medieval days it was an impregnable fortress. The main towers had underground connections, water pipes, wells, cellars, vast stores of food and gunpowder. Some of the secret passages led to underwater locks along the Moskva River. Others corkscrewed out beyond the walls, under Red Square, and into the tangle of buildings then known as Khitai Gorod, or the Chinese City.

There's not a dramatic event in Russian history which did not happen—or echo loudly— over the turreted Kremlin walls. Here the little wilderness fiefdom that was to grow into the

KHITAI GOROD

powerful principality of Muscovy took root. Here
on April 4, 1147, Prince Yuri Dolgoruki (Longarms) chanced to pause on the way back to his
home at nearby Suzdal.

A little settlement stood on the brow of the hill.
It belonged to a boyar, or nobleman, named
Stepan Kuchko. Prince Longarms, or so the story
goes, told the boyar he wanted to "enjoy his hos-
pitality." Kuchko wasn't feeling hospitable and
gave him a rude reply. That made Longarms

angry. He ordered his followers to drown Kuchko in a pond. Then he took Kuchko's wife and daughter prisoner, seized the land, and built a wooden stockade around it, very much like those the pioneers in America built against the Indians.

The wooden stockade was called a *krim* or a *krem,* which is an old Greek word for fortress. That is why today it is known as the Kremlin or, in Russian, Kreml.

After Longarms seized the settlement it apparently was still called Kuchkovo, for its former owner, for a long time. There is even yet a little neighborhood in Moscow called Kuchkovo. As for the name Moscow, nobody really knows where that word comes from, although Russian scholars for generations have been searching through the old archives for some clue.

If we could turn the clock of history back to medieval times, we would find many a European city that looked like the Kremlin compound. It was a walled city just as the "City" in London once was. Or the "Île de France" in Paris. The London walls all came tumbling down centuries past and the "City" has become the London financial district. The walls are gone in Paris, too. But here in Moscow they still stand. In the Kremlin, preserved in stone and masonry, can be found almost the whole story of Russia. When we walk

IVAN THE GREAT

across the great squares inside the Kremlin compound, we are treading on the stage where some of the great epics of Russia were played out. Much of this history is stained by blood, shadowed by deceit, and haunted by despotism. The poet Alfred Rimbaud once said that "the Princes of Moscow gained their ends by intrigue, corruption, the purchase of conscience, servility to the Khans, perfidy to their equals, murder and treachery." Another commentator once said, "The throne of England descends according to the principle of primogeniture; that of Russia by regicide." Those are strong words, but the tale of the Kremlin has not been a pretty one.

CATHERINE THE
GREAT

The great builders of the Kremlin were Ivan Kalita (his name means John Moneybags), Ivan III, Catherine II, and Nicholas I. Ivan Moneybags lived in the early fourteenth century. He rose to power by acting as agent for the Mongol despots in collecting tribute from his fellow Russians. Russia fell under Mongol domination in 1240. In that year Batyi, the great Tatar general, conquered Kiev. It was not until 1552, with the victory of Ivan IV over the Golden Horde at Kazan, that the Tatar yoke was finally lifted. Ivan III was known as Ivan the Great. He was the first Russian ruler to challenge the reign of the Tatars.

He called himself "Autocrat and Sovereign of All the Russias." Catherine was also called "the Great." She lived at the time of the American and French Revolutions. She was a liberal ruler until the revolutions frightened her back into tyranny. Nicholas I was probably the most autocratic of all the Czars. He ruled for thirty years from 1825 to 1855.

During Stalin's life no one was permitted to walk freely about the Kremlin. Each year a few foreigners and a few Russians were taken through the grounds on special guided tours. Many persons lived their whole lives in Moscow and never got to see the Kremlin. After Stalin died all this changed. The forbidden gates swung open. Now millions of persons every year visit the Kremlin, most of them casual strollers who wander through the great squares, inspect the ancient cathedrals, sun themselves in the rose gardens, or patronize the Kremlin theaters.

But the Kremlin is not just a place for sightseers. It is the seat of the Soviet Government. When Lenin moved the capital from Petrograd in 1918, he set up offices in the Kremlin. Indeed, he actually lived there in a four-room suite that has been preserved just as it was in his day. Stalin lived and worked there too. After his death the Soviet leaders stopped living in the Kremlin.

LENIN

Instead, they built themselves a row of identical houses on a high hill overlooking the Moskva River, not far from the new Moscow University. But they kept their offices in the Kremlin. Strollers on the grounds often see the Soviet rulers, coming and going, in their long black limousines.

The great rooms of the Kremlin palaces were locked up, dusty and unused during Stalin's day. Now the government uses them for holiday fetes. Lovely St. George's Hall, all white and gold and marble, on whose walls may be read in golden letters the names of every holder of St. George's Cross, the highest Czarist decoration for bravery, is the scene of big diplomatic receptions.

CROWNS FROM THE 17TH AND 18TH CENTURIES

All day long visitors throng the ancient Armory, where the imperial treasure of old Russia is on display. Here are the Hall of Armor, the Hall of Arms, the Hall of Crowns and the Hall of Silver—a collection of objects of gold, of silver, of pearls, diamonds, emeralds, and rubies which some experts believe more valuable than those of the Tower of London or the Louvre in Paris.

Here are preserved the legendary "Crown" of Monomakh, a curious cap of metal, jewels, and fur said to have been worn by one of the early rulers of Kiev; the jeweled orb of Monomakh, symbol of Russian power; the jewel-studded crowns of Kazan (worn by Ivan IV after his victory at Kazan in 1552); of Michael Romanov, the first of the dynasty; the silk and gold-threaded gowns of Catherine II; the boots of Peter the Great, as tall as a small man (Peter was six feet, eight inches tall); the throne of the Czar Alexis, sparkling with more than two thousand diamonds; the crowns of Georgia and Armenia; vestments of patriarchs of the Orthodox Church so heavy with pearls that only a strong man could

THE GRANOVITAYA
PALACE

wear them; the double throne of Peter the Great and his weakling brother, Ivan.

There are thousands of valued objects in this greatest of the Russian national museums. Here are the gold and silver services presented to the Czars by all the crowned heads of Europe; the miraculously ingenious Easter eggs made for the imperial family to give as presents by the famous firm of Fabergé (each egg contains a "surprise"— for instance, a tiny working model in platinum and gold of the Trans-Siberian Express); magnificent *bratiny,* traditional Russian loving cups whose

THE CATHEDRAL OF
THE ANNUNCIATION

name comes from the word *brat*, meaning brother; *kovsh*, boat-shaped bowls for beer; *charky*, small, embossed cups for vodka.

Many of these remarkable objects were made by the skilled artisans of the Armory. Until dissolved by Peter the Great in 1711 the Armory constituted the court workshops, the finest group of artists in Russia and one of the finest in Europe.

Today in the Kremlin there is a constant movement of crowds. Some are visiting the exquisite theater that Stalin kept for his own use but that is now open to the public. There are plays there every night, put on by some of the best companies in Russia. And in 1962 a remarkable new building, the Kremlin Palace of Congresses, was erected. It is a beautiful white structure in the most modern style of architecture, all glass and flat façades. Inside there's a theater with seats for 6500, fast-moving escalators, a restaurant and roof garden on the top floor, lounges, and refreshment stands.

Here world congresses and conventions are held. When no meetings are in progress, the stage is used by the ballet company of the Bolshoi Theater.

At New Year's time the Kremlin becomes a winter fairyland for children. Carnivals are set up inside the ancient walls. Music blares from loudspeakers. Small youngsters slide down great Russian bears carved of solid ice. Teen-agers dance to modern bands. There are movies and games, toys and presents. Grandfather Frost (Russia's stand-in for Santa Claus) is on hand. So is the Snegurichka, or Snow Maiden. The old fortress looks more like Disneyland than a scene of dread and terror.

And that, of course, is what the new leaders of the Soviet want—a benevolent image for an ancient symbol of tyranny.

A JEWELED EASTER
EGG

IV. A Passion for Bells

FIRE, not enemy besiegers, was the greatest threat to medieval Moscow. Indeed, the early history of the city is little more than a catalogue of fires. Some of the more notable conflagrations occurred in 1177, 1237, 1238, 1331, 1354, 1365, 1384, 1493 (probably the worst of all), 1547 (second only to the fire of 1493), 1737, and finally in 1812 at the time of Napoleon's invasion. And there were many, many more. Red Square was known for several hundred years as Pozharny Square—the Square of the Fire. In Moscow back streets you can still see a few of the old fire towers where watchers used to stand guard, day and night, to alert the patrols when fire broke out in the wooden city.

Again and again the Kremlin has been rebuilt. Small wonder that only relics of the "oaken Kremlin" of Ivan Moneybags remains. One Moscow building that dated back to his time stood until recently, however. This was the little church of

The Saviour in the Woods. It had been built on the Borovitsky Hill, overlooking the Moskva River, in the 1200's. It was a wood structure, and in 1329 Ivan Moneybags erected a stone church on the spot, incorporating the old wooden church into the new.

This ancient church survived to the mid-1930's, when it was finally torn down by the Communists while they were rebuilding part of the Great Kremlin Palace to provide a meeting hall for their Congress, the Supreme Soviet.

In recent years excavators have dug up bits of the old oaken wall that surrounded the Kremlin in 1339. These pieces are on display in the Moscow Museum of Planning and Reconstruction.

If we look in vain for survivals of the old wooden Kremlin, there's no such trouble about the Kremlin of Ivan the Great, the medieval fortress with its complex of palaces and churches. This was constructed about the time when Columbus was setting off on his journey of discovery. Those were the years when Muscovy was coming to power, throwing off the Mongols, consolidating the Russian state. As the Czars grew rich and powerful, the Kremlin flourished with magnificence. The great treasures of the Armory Palace began to pile up. Much of the Kremlin that still stands was built in that period—the great Spassky

and Nikolsky gates, most of the lovely high walls
of pink brick (in those days they were carefully
painted white), the Tainitskaya (Secret) Tower
which had a spring of fresh water in its cellar, the
Beklemishevskaya Tower (a prison tower where
state criminals were beheaded and the bodies interred in crypts) the Vodovzodnaya Tower (a
secret underground pumping station) and the
great Arsenal Tower. This was one of the out-
standing forts of Europe. It possessed an inex-
haustible spring that is running to this day and
still gives the Kremlin engineers drainage head-
aches.

Today you can walk all around the Kremlin on
dry land. Even on the side facing the Moskva
River the Kremlin walls stand back a hundred
yards or more from the water line. But until the
eighteenth century the whole Kremlin was a
moated fort. The moat was thirty to forty feet
deep and hundred to a hundred twenty feet wide.
You entered the grounds by huge bridges that
could be drawn up, completely enclosing the
Kremlin for defense. This was possible because of
the Neglinnaya River, whose waters were di-
verted to form canals along the west, the north,
and the east sides of the Kremlin. The Moskva
River provided a natural defense for the south
wall. Gradually as the nature of warfare changed

the moat sank into disuse. By the time Peter moved the capital from Moscow to Petersburg in 1712, it had been abandoned. The Neglinnaya River eventually was channeled into underground pipes and stone passages, something like the sewers of Paris described by Victor Hugo in *Les Miserables*. The Neglinnaya bed eventually became the Alexandrovsky Gardens, a quiet maze of flowers and paths. There along the western walls of the Kremlin mothers and nursemaids sun their babies and in wintertime little children test out new skis on the gentle slopes.

At the center of the Kremlin is Cathedral Square. Here is Assumption Cathedral, where every Russian sovereign was crowned from the fifteenth century onwards. It is Russia's Westminster Abbey. The bearded boyars who saw it for the first time in the fifteenth century cast themselves down in awe and called it "the see of heaven." Beside it stands the Cathedral of the Archangel Michael, where every Czar until the day of Peter the Great was buried—excepting only Boris Godunov. Ivan the Terrible lies here. So do his two sons, one murdered by his father in a fit of insane rage, the other his feeble-minded successor. Across the square stands the Cathedral of the Annunciation, in which the Czars were baptized and married.

Nothing delighted the old Russians more than bells. Some Russians came close to madness in their fondness for the pealing of the chimes. They gave up anything for bells. The right to ring the bells was not a duty but a great privilege. Rich men beggared themselves to give bells to the churches. Many churches possessed bells of gold and silver, which powerful Czars often seized and melted down to finance their wars. When the inhabitants of the town of Uglich rang their bell to rally a demonstration against Ivan the Terrible, the cruel Czar executed two hundred boyars, and exiled the Uglich bell to Siberia, where it remained for two hundred years.

The Ivan the Great tower stands in Cathedral Square as a monument to the Russian love of bells. Until Stalin's skyscrapers were built, this 270-foot tower was the tallest structure in Moscow. It had a peal of thirty-three bells, including the most famous bell in Russia, the Novgorod Bell. Novgorod was one of the most ancient and powerful cities in Russia, a center of free trade and free thought. Ivan the Great finally crushed Novgorod and made it submit to Moscow. As a symbol of Novgorod's submission he seized the Novgorod Bell, transported it to Moscow, and hung it in the Kremlin.

When the Kremlin bells were sounded to cele-

**THE BELL TOWER OF
IVAN THE GREAT**

brate some great victory or feast day, the first to ring was the "town bell of Moscow," housed in a high cupola just beside the Ivan the Great tower. Then the Ivan bells rang out and the peal was taken up by the bells of Moscow's "forty times forty" churches. The "forty times forty" phrase was figurative, not literal. There were never more than about five hundred churches in Moscow, but these were enough to send the sound over the city like waves of a musical hurricane.

Boris Godunov, whose strange career as Czar of all the Russias has been celebrated in a famous opera, built the Ivan the Great tower in 1600. After the tower was knocked slightly askew in Napoleon's shelling of the Kremlin in 1812, the Russians began to call it "Ivan the Tipsy." Boris Godunov also ordered the casting of the Czar Kolokol, the Emperor of Bells, which he intended to mount in the Ivan the Great tower. This was the biggest bell in the world. It weighed 288 tons originally. When it was cracked by fire, its size was increased in the recasting to 423 tons. Before it could be mounted, fire again broke out and a piece the size of a barn door chipped off. The

THE CZAR OF BELLS

huge bell tumbled to earth and lay there, half-buried in the ground, for 125 years. Finally in 1835 it was fished up with great difficulty and mounted for exhibit.

The Czar of Bells stands beside the Czar Pushka, or Czar of Cannons. This monstrous forty-ton cannon was cast in 1586 for Czar Feodor, the feeble-minded son of Ivan the Terrible. Feodor wanted the largest cannon in the world. He got it, but when the weapon had been cast no one ever dared fire it for fear it would blow up. It was built to fire a cannon ball a yard in diameter.

The useless bell and the useless cannon stand side by side in the Kremlin, monuments to Russia's thwarted gigantomania.

Perhaps it is because the passion for bells ran

THE CZAR OF
CANNONS

so high in Russia's past that they are practically banned in the Russia of today. Bells never sound in Soviet Moscow except for the chimes of the Spassky clock tower, which ring out the national anthem at midnight. The Kremlin cathedral bells are never sounded, and those of the Moscow churches only at Easter.

Facing Cathedral Square is the Granovitaya Palata, or Palace of Facets. Its diamond-cut stone walls are very much like those of the famous Pitti Palace in Florence. This was a crowning achievement of Ivan the Great. It was in this palace that Ivan the Terrible celebrated his victory over the Tatars at Kazan, which finally freed Russia from Mongol domination. Here Peter the Great celebrated his victory over the Swedes at Poltava in 1709.

From this palace access to Cathedral Square was given by the famous Krasnoye Kryltso, the "Beautiful Entrance" or "Red Staircase," depending on how you translate the Russian words. This was the main entryway to the old palace. Its walls were decorated with gold leaf and on state occasions its ancient stones were covered with a red carpet sixteen feet wide. Over the years the stones literally were stained with blood.

From the Red Staircase, Peter the Great, then only ten years old, watched the Streltsy, the picked Palace Guard, murder his mother's uncle before his eyes. Here he stood again when he was proclaimed Czar seven years later, having put down another revolt of the Streltsy with executions as bloodcurdling as those he had witnessed as a child. These executions are the subject of one of the most famous paintings in Moscow's great national Tretyakov Gallery, a work by Surikov called *The Morning of the Execution of the Streltsy*. It depicts the throngs in Red Square as the doomed men are brought out to the execution platform.

The Red Staircase was often rebuilt. Finally in 1935, when Stalin was carrying out extensive changes in the Kremlin, it was ripped down, possibly because it was too forcible a reminder of the terrors of the past.

The Granovitaya Palata and the Terem, with which it is connected, form the oldest surviving residence quarters in the Kremlin. Once there were many houses and palaces for noblemen and clergy in the Kremlin. But all of the houses and monasteries have been taken down, many of them since the Communists came to power. In the ancient rooms of the Granovitaya Palata, with low ceilings, windows of blue, orange, red, and purple glass, great tile stoves that reach to the ceiling, gloomy murals of saints and devils, twisting staircases, and gold-decorated reception rooms, the early Czars from the time of Ivan the Great lived, banqueted and worshiped, worked and died. Here is the Room of the Cross, a waiting room for boyars and petitioners. Here is the Golden Room, the Czar's working chamber. Sometimes he sat at an ordinary table, sometimes on a throne. From the Golden Room a window looks out on the square. From the window each day a long box was lowered. Into it any Russian, noble or pauper, could put a letter with a promise that the Czar himself would read the petition. Did the Czar heed his subjects' complaints? Apparently not. To this day the expression "putting it in the long box" means, in Russian, to pigeonhole a matter.

The Terem was the women's quarters of the palace. From the Mongols the early Russians acquired the habit of keeping their wives and daughters hidden away almost as in a harem. The custom gradually died, particularly after Peter's Westernizing campaigns. But under Stalin it was revived. The wives of Communist leaders never appeared in public with their husbands. Wives of the top Communists didn't go to state receptions. They didn't attend the theater with their husbands. No one even knew whether a Bolshevik Communist leader was married or not. But with the rise of Khrushchev this changed. Mrs.

Khrushchev has often appeared at her husband's side. She has traveled with him to America. The other Soviet wives have come out of seclusion as well.

The tendency of later years was toward a breaking down of barriers as the Soviet Government sought to tear away the veil of secrecy and mystery which had surrounded the Kremlin and its inmates.

V. A Gathering Place
for 500 Years

LATE AT NIGHT during early November the central streets of Moscow rumble with the movement of heavy tanks and guns. Truckloads of troops swing through the squares at 2 and 3 A.M. Sometimes, during the day, flights of jet planes swoop low over Red Square with a roar of engines like thunder. Newcomers to Moscow might think that a revolution was in progress, but they are quickly set straight. The planes and troops and tanks are just practicing for the celebration of the anniversary of November 7, the day the Bolsheviks seized power in 1917. The same practice goes on just before May Day, the other big Soviet holiday.

On November 7 anyone who has to work gets up early because he must get to his job before all ordinary traffic in the center of the city is halted at 7 A.M. By eight o'clock security troops stand guard on all approaches to Red Square. By nine o'clock diplomats, high officials, and the other lucky invitation holders are hurrying into the square, and by ten o'clock the plaza is filled with troops. A six-hundred-man band stands before Lenin's Mausoleum. The Soviet leaders take their places on the reviewing stand atop the tomb. Saluting cannon roar from behind the Kremlin wall. The commanding general reviews the troops and mounts the reviewing stand to take the salute. The band strikes up Glinka's *Hail to the Czar* (now retitled *Hail to the People*). And the spectacle is under way. For hours the square, draped with bunting, banners, and slogans—"Workers of the World Unite," "Glory to the Soviet State," "Hail Unbreakable Friendship of Communist Peoples" —echoes to the tramp of soldiers, the roar of armored vehicles, the rumble of cannon, and the shouts of hundreds of thousands of citizens who participate in a "spontaneous demonstration" for the Communist regime.

When Stalin's death was announced on the morning of March 5, 1953, a handful of people appeared in the middle of Red Square. They stood outside the Spassky Gate waiting in silent expectation. Moment by moment the throng grew. Soon there were a hundred people waiting. Then a thousand. Then two thousand. Three thousand. A little later long lines of police troops relentlessly moved the people out of the square.

Why had the people come? What did they expect? Perhaps they could not have said themselves. Probably it was instinct. For nearly five hundred years the people of Moscow have gathered in Red Square at times of triumph, despair, tragedy, and celebration. When the Nazi troops were hammering at the very suburbs of Moscow in November, 1941, Siberian reinforcements for the Soviet front paraded through Red Square before Stalin and the Russian leaders. When the Soviet armies finally began to turn back the Nazi tide, Stalin had mounted salute guns behind the Kremlin wall and on the roofs of the great arcade that faces the square. Each time the Red Army recaptured a Soviet city—Kharkov, Rostov, Smolensk, Kiev, Sevastopol or Odessa—a salute was ordered. Tired, worn, half-starved, the people of Moscow turned out to watch the guns fire cascades of rockets, red and green, gold and purple, high into the air as loudspeakers crashed forth with the Soviet national anthem.

When Moscow celebrated its eight hundredth anniversary in 1947, a dazzle of lights outlined every curlicue of the Kremlin walls and turrets. At night a million people, even possibly two million, gathered in the square. Again the guns sent up showers of rockets. Aerial searchlights punctured the darkness. High above the crowd, dangling from a blimp, appeared a hundred-foot transparency of Stalin in lifelike colors.

Here in Red Square the stage has been set for many of the great moments in Russian history. From the ebb and flow of the crowds we learn the character of the Russian people and the temper of the regime under which they are living.

In Stalin's day people did not walk freely in the square. They were afraid. The police kept them moving. All night long curtained limousines swished in and out of the Spassky gate with a clang of alarm bells, a flash of signals, and a frantic salute by the police. The lights in the Kremlin buildings blazed until 4 A.M. or 5 A.M. What went on no one knew—or cared to know. It was too dangerous.

Across the square stood one of the biggest buildings in Europe, 825 feet long, 300 feet deep, and 3 stories high. Once it had been a huge department store. But Stalin didn't like to have shoppers on Red Square. So many ordinary people so near at hand made him nervous. He closed it down, and the great gray buildings were turned over to small departments of the government for offices.

It was as a symbol of the change his death produced that the buildings were renovated in 1954 and transformed into GUM, the biggest and busiest retail store in the Communist world. More than 300,000 customers jam the glass and ornamental-iron corridors of GUM on weekend shopping days. There's a fountain playing in the center aisle, a fashion show on one of the upper floors, a jewelry store with thousand-dollar diamond rings, a lost-and-found bureau for strayed children, and a loudspeaker system to advertise the latest bargains. You can buy a new suit or a

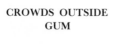

CROWDS OUTSIDE
GUM

silk dress on credit terms. But you may have to wait three months for delivery on a new TV set.

Trade is no stranger to the Red Square. When Ivan the Great created the square in 1493 by clearing out all the low-lying buildings next to the Kremlin moat, trading stalls sprang up near the Moskva River. There were *kharchevoy ryad,* where food was sold; *shaposhny ryad,* which dealt in hats; *medovy ryad,* which sold wine and mead; *ptichey* for chickens and geese; *ikonny* for ikons; and other stalls for rugs, firearms, silver, pewter, brass, and leather.

Along the Kremlin moat and on the eastern side of Red Square there were also wooden bazaars. Just beside the Spassky gates stalls for book- and printsellers stood all through the eighteenth century. These flimsy quarters often burned to the ground in Moscow's frequent fires. More permanent shops were built, but deep mud in the spring and heavy winter snowdrifts interfered with trade.

Finally, permanent arcades were built on the eastern side of the square. What is today the big GUM store was built in the 1870's and 1880's. Its single glass roof was the largest ever installed.

At the entrance of Red Square there are two big red brick buildings in the ornately decorated Russian style. One houses the State Historical

Museum. The other was the State Duma, or Council, building before the Revolution. Now it is the Lenin Museum. Until the early 1930's there stood between the two buildings the gemlike little Chapel of the Iberian Virgin, built in 1669, one of the holiest places in Russia. When the Czar returned to Moscow after an absence, he always stopped first to pray at this chapel before entering the Kremlin. The ikon of the chapel, depicting the Virgin Mary, was reputed to have miraculous powers. For a suitable contribution a Moscow merchant or prince could arrange for the ikon to be sent to his home for a few hours. Often this was done when there was sickness in a wealthy family, for the ikon was said work cures. It was carried about Moscow in a special curtained carriage that was always recognizable because the footmen rode with their heads uncovered. While the Iberian ikon was away on a visit, an exact duplicate was hung in its place.

The chapel was a victim of the Communist regime. It was torn down to make it easier to move troops to the Kremlin in case of a popular uprising. On the wall where the chapel formerly stood was placed a plaque with the words of Karl Marx: "Religion is the opiate of the masses."

Perhaps from a sense of embarrassment the inscription was taken down from the wall by Sta-

THE STATE
HISTORICAL MUSEUM

lin's successors. But the Iberian chapel, of course, could not be restored.

Five days a week, winter and summer, a long line of people snakes across Red Square, carefully disciplined by uniformed policemen and plainclothes men each wearing a red band on his arm which says, "Patrol."

These are visitors to the severely plain, square, dark red Mausoleum, constructed of Ukrainian granite, black and gray labradorite, and Canadian porphyry, where the body of Vladimir I. Lenin, the founder of the Soviet state, rests. Lenin died in January 1924, on a bitterly cold day in a little village just outside Moscow where he had been recuperating from a series of strokes. His body was embalmed by a secret process and placed in the mausoleum. There it has been on view continuously ever since—except for the war years, when it was taken to the interior for safety's sake. Those who have seen the body at intervals over the years say it shows little sign of change.

When Stalin died in 1953, his body was also

THE LINE OUTSIDE LENIN'S TOMB

embalmed and put to rest beside that of Lenin. The words above the mausoleum entrance were changed to read, "Lenin/Stalin." But in 1962, after many of Stalin's crimes had been publicly denounced by Khrushchev and others, the body was removed from the mausoleum and buried under a simple gravestone in a little cemetery that lies near the Kremlin wall, just behind the tomb. The single name "Lenin" was restored to the stone above the mausoleum entrance.

In the tiny graveyard and in urns set in to the wall of the Kremlin behind the mausoleum are buried most of the important Communist leaders —except for those whom Stalin executed. Some of the less important figures are buried in the cemetery of the Novo Devichy (New Maiden) Monastery. There in a simple, tasteful grave is buried Stalin's wife, Nadezhda Alleluyeva, who is believed to have taken her own life after a bitter argument with her husband in 1932 over his arbitrary methods. In the Kremlin wall there are interred several foreigners, including a number of Americans. Among them are John Reed, a young American newspaperman who was a friend of Lenin and whose *Ten Days That Shook the World* is the classic eyewitness account of the Bolshevik Revolution, and William (Big Bill) Haywood, an American anarchist or I.W.W. who jumped bail in the United States and fled to Russia.

VI. Promenades and Spectacles

AMONG the people of Eastern Europe nothing is more popular than a formal promenade. Moscow's citizens are no exception to this rule. The *gulyanye,* as the promenade is called, has been a favorite Russian pastime since the dawn of history. To the Slav peoples a promenade doesn't just mean a stroll in the park. It is something special, marked by street entertainments and booths, dancing, merriment, and gaiety.

After the big parades on May Day and November 7 everyone in Moscow turns out into the streets. Traffic is barred from the central squares. Bands play on elevated platforms. Movies are shown on outdoor screens. Ice-cream girls do a rushing business in Eskimo Pies and ice-cream cones. Older people stroll about in their best clothes, stopping now and then to watch young men and women play a Russian version of "London Bridge Is Falling Down." Dancers in national costumes, bright with embroidery, throw them-

selves into the wild Cossack *kazatski*. Some of the
youngsters take up rock 'n' roll and the twist. At
night there are fireworks in the parks.

In June, Moscow celebrates the "white nights,"
when in this northern latitude the sun doesn't set
until almost midnight and begins to rise again a
little after two in the morning. It never really gets
dark. You can read a newspaper out of doors at
midnight. At one o'clock the streets are still filled
with a pale light that gives the city an atmosphere
of mystery. This is the end of the school term.
High-school and college boys and girls, the boys
in their best dark suits, the girls in billowy white
dresses, come down to the big Moscow restaurants. They eat dinner and then, as the clocks
strike midnight, drift out into the streets. There is
little traffic and the air is warm and soft. They
link arms and stroll down the center of the streets,
singing old Moscow songs. As the night wears on,
they join with other students and gradually con-
gregate in Red Square just as the sun from over
the Moskva River begins to tint with rose and
gold the turrets and domes of the Kremlin. There
beside the ancient Russian walls their voices ring
out in a swelling chorus as thousands join in the
song fest. Then, as the sun rises higher, they
slowly wander back through the quiet Moscow
streets toward home. Before Stalin's death the

young people were not permitted to gather in
Red Square. Now each year the number grows
larger and larger. It has become the traditional
way to celebrate the end of the school year.

In ancient times the spring *gulyanye* in Red
Square took another form. It was celebrated on
Willow Saturday, just before Palm Sunday. In
the early 1800's everyone in Moscow turned out
for it—the noblemen and their wives, the merchants and their families, and the common people. The wealthy rode out in their most expensive
carriages, swinging down Red Square to the
Spassky Gate, over the bridge and through the
Kremlin, and then out again. Countless specta-
tors thronged the streets and squares. The *gulyanye* apparently had its origin in an even earlier
ceremony, a Lenten observance in which the
Czar, walking on foot, led a donkey by the bridle.
The Orthodox Patriarch was mounted on the
donkey. They came out of the Kremlin by the
Spassky Gate, circled the lower end of Red
Square, and then returned to the Kremlin, where
the Patriarch offered a Mass. In the middle of the
nineteenth century the holiday was transferred
out of Red Square to Tchaikovsky Street, the
broad boulevard where the U. S. Embassy now
stands. By this time it was a kind of winter fair or
carnival with booths, outdoor restaurants, and en-

tertainment. It is no longer held there, but a similar carnival is held about the same time in the Central Gorky Park.

For centuries Red Square was the scene of incredible spectacles, many of which have left some mark behind them. At the southern end of the square, near St. Basil's Cathedral, stands a round stone platform. It is quite unadorned. At holiday times it is filled with red banners. At night floodlights turn the platform into a bouquet of gigantic blood-red flowers that seem to grow out of the old gray stones. Well they might. This circular platform is the Lobnoye Mesto, the Place of the Skull. It was the execution site where hundreds upon hundreds of heads were lopped off during medieval times.

In every medieval city of Europe the central market was used as the place for punishment and execution. Red Square was no exception. Executions were carried out here as late as 1727. Not only were victims beheaded. They were hanged, broken on wheels, buried alive, burned in iron cages, torn to pieces with sharp hooks, pulled apart on stretchers, quartered, whipped to death with the knout, and scalded to death in boiling water. Molten lead was poured into the throats of traitors. Unfaithful wives were buried to the neck and left to die. Victims were tortured for hours before thousands of persons before being burned at the stake. Heads were impaled on pikes and left in the square for days and weeks as a warning to others. Corpses were chained to stakes until packs of mongrel dogs gnawed them to pieces.

Ivan the Terrible was particularly noted for his executions and tortures. Once, after he had fled Moscow and left the city defenseless to be ravaged, looted, and burned by the Mongols, he finally returned to his capital, mounted the Lobnoye Mesto, and confessed his sins to his people, crying, tearing his hair, beating his breast, and ripping his clothes in humiliation. It should be remembered that Ivan lived in an age of cruelty and barbarism. Everywhere in Europe atrocities were carried out in the name of authority. Henry VIII of England and Queen Elizabeth were Ivan's contemporaries. So were the authors of the Spanish Inquisition. In Russia, Ivan was regarded as a man in advance of his times. The great English trader Sir Richard Chancellor came to Moscow in Ivan's reign. Ivan was known to his people as the "English Czar." He dreamed of marrying Queen Elizabeth I, and when she tactfully rejected his suit he bid for the hand of Lady Mary Hastings. Once when Ivan thought he might be driven from the Russian throne he arranged with Elizabeth to take refuge in England.

Red Square, of course, was more than simply an outdoor chamber of horrors. Peter the Great set up in 1702 a wooden theater beside the Nikolsky Gate close to where the State Historical Museum now stands. It was the first theater in Russia open to the general public. It put on twelve-act plays. During the long intermissions, comedians, jugglers, and magicians appeared. Some of the twelve-act plays took a whole week to perform at the rate of three or four acts a day. In the big fire of 1737 the House of Comedy, as the theater was called, burned down. It was not rebuilt.

The other end of the square, close to St. Basil's, was always a scene of lively activity. In addition to shops and bazaars there were stands for food—*pirogi,* meat pies; *kolachi,* twists of white bread; *kvas,* the mild, effervescent drink made of fermented rye bread which is loved by Russians in the summertime. The appearance of the *kvas* wagons, round, barrel-like affairs, on the Moscow streets, with their white-aproned girl attendants, is still a sign that summer is really at hand. Other stalls sold *sbeeten,* hot mead, a strong fermented drink made of honey. In ancient times hot mead was a great favorite in Scandinavia and Anglo-Saxon England as well.

There were comedians, acrobats, blind beggars, and prostitutes in the square. Here, too, you

found trained bears. Performances by bears were one of the favorite amusements of old Russia in spite of efforts by the Orthodox Church to discourage them on grounds of immorality.

Here, too, there were *kabaki,* low public houses, serving vodka and strong drink and catering to the riffraff of the town. The most notorious of the *kabaki* was known as the *podpushkoi,* which means "under the cannon." It was located under a row of cannon mounted outside the Kremlin walls. This place was crowded with naked and half-naked unfortunates who had sold their clothes for drink or food. Foreigners visiting Moscow invariably were brought to see this strange and horrible spectacle. Maxim Gorky's famous play *The Lower Depths* is set in a place like this that was located in the 1880's in the Khitrovka market.

The square bristled with pickpockets, thieves, cutthroats, escaped criminals, police spies, and counterspies. In the big Zemstvo, or Council, building, which stood where the State Historical Museum is now located, there was a special police station with underground prison cells. These were always filled with victims seized from the busy crowds in the square.

Before the days of newspapers foreigners and diplomats as well as merchants and courtiers came to the square to hear the news. The *prikazes* or edicts of the Czars were read out here by the town crier. When Peter the Great moved the capital of Russia to St. Petersburg, Red Square began to change. After the great fire of Moscow in 1812 at the time of Napoleon's invasion it never regained its former character. The shops and trading stalls were pulled down. The old Kremlin moat was turned into a garden. The street peddlers and thieves were chased away. The square began to gain its present appearance.

But it had not seen the last of dramatic events. When the Bolshevik uprising broke out on November 7, 1917, supporters of the Kerensky provisional government, many of them officers and young cadets, held the Kremlin. Fierce fighting went on for eight days. Barricades were thrown up in Red Square. Cannon echoed on both sides. More than five hundred persons were killed in what turned out to be the fiercest battle of the Bolshevik *coup d'état*. The revolutionary troops killed in the fighting are buried in two "brothers' graves," just behind the Lenin Mausoleum.

Today Red Square is a peaceful, busy place. Tourists throng into the Kremlin, a long line of visitors moves through Lenin's tomb, and tens of thousands of shoppers bustle in and out of the GUM department store.

But if dramatic events again come to Russia, we may be sure that they will echo loudly as in the past over the great sea of gray paving stones.

AN OLD PRINT OF NAPOLEON WATCHING MOSCOW BURN

ST. BASIL'S CATHEDRAL

VII. THE LEGEND OF ST. BASIL'S

THERE is a legend that after the Cathedral of St. Basil's was finished Ivan the Terrible summoned its Italian architect and demanded to know whether he could build another church as beautiful as this one. The architect replied that he could. Ivan then had him blinded so that no other monarch might possess a miracle surpassing that of St. Basil's.

When you first see St. Basil's, with its bulblike

towers, blossoming like giant tulips across the expanse of Red Square, you blink. It cannot be. You never have seen anything like this. No church in the West—not St. Patrick's, St. Mark's, or Notre Dame—compares with it. The towers are every color—blue, green, purple, yellow, orange, red, gold. They are of every shape—tall, squat, thin, fat, round, pointed. Some are decorated. Some are not. Some are candy-striped. Some are mottled. Some are twisted like crullers. Others bulge like cream puffs.

It is easy to believe that the eccentric Ivan might have ordered the architect of St. Basil's to be blinded, or, as another version has it, beheaded.

Plausible as the stories seem, they are not true. The architect of St. Basil's was not an Italian. The church was designed by two Russians, architects from ancient Pskov, named Barmia and Posnik Yakovlev. They were neither tortured nor beheaded. They were richly rewarded by Ivan for their genius.

Their creation has been compared to "an immense dragon," a "brilliant bird of paradise," a "great explosion," a "gigantic bouquet." Or even to the crystals of a madrepore, or giant coral plant. Certainly St. Basil's is one of the great architectural monuments of the world and one of enormous meaning to Russia.

The church is a truly national shrine. It was

erected by Ivan between 1553 and 1560 to commemorate Russia's victories over the Golden Horde of Mongols at Kazan and Astrakhan. These victories once and for all freed Russia from the thralldom imposed by the invaders from the East.

As such the cathedral is, in effect, a monument to Russian independence and Russian national spirit. Its strange form was not a matter of chance. It was dictated by the purpose of the cathedral. The building consists of a central church that is surrounded by eight smaller churches, each connected with the main church and each dedicated to a saint on whose day fell one of the victories over the Mongols. The special chapel to St. Basil the Blessed, a mendicant, prophet, and miracle worker, one of those simple men much venerated in Russia as "Christ's fools," was added a few years later.

One must be a Russian to appreciate the full significance of Ivan's victory over the Mongols. Ancient Russia, which had centered about the capital of Kiev, was one of Europe's great powers. Its culture, based on Greek heritage, equaled or surpassed those of many Western nations. Then suddenly the curtain came down. Thousands of miles to the east in remote, unheard-of Mongolia appeared the greatest conquerer the world has ever known, Genghis Khan. His horsemen swept to the west, driving all before them. His vanguards penetrated to the vicinity of the Sea of Azov. There the first battle between the Russians and the Mongols was fought, June 16, 1228.

The Mongols defeated the Russians but did not press their advantage. They retreated back into their Asian fastness, probably because they received news of the death of Genghis Khan about this time. But soon a nephew, Batyi, took up the battle. In 1237, he crossed the Volga with an army of 300,000 cavalry and in 1240 annihilated Kiev. The Mongol horde swept into Poland, Hungary, Bohemia, and Austria. It even reached the Adriatic Sea. Europe trembled.

The Russian state was virtually destroyed. Only small fortress cities far to the northwest, deep in the forest and marsh, like Moscow, Vladimir, Novgorod, and Suzdal, survived precariously. They were often attacked and burned to the ground by the Mongols. Their men were slaughtered. Their women by the thousand were marched off to Asia and Turkey as slaves and concubines.

Southern Russia, the rich and fertile lands around Kiev, became a desert. The sites of cities were marked by heaps of skulls. For miles about there was no human life. The Russian nation vanished from the map.

It was in these tragic circumstances that Moscow began its slow rise to prominence. Had not Moscow been so remote, so poor, so small, so inconsequential, so difficult for the Mongol horsemen to reach, it would not have survived. But with the aid of crafty rulers like Ivan Moneybags, who was willing to submit to the Tatars, collect tribute from his own people for the khans, do their bidding, and, meanwhile, feather his own nest, Moscow began to grow. As the famous Russian democrat Alexander Hertzen put it: "Moscow grew under the Tatar yoke and took possession of Russia, not by virtue of its own merits but through the insufficiency of the other provinces."

But Moscow did possess certain advantages. It was located on the main water route between the Baltic and the south at a time when most goods traveled by water. Trade moved down the Volkhov River to Novgorod and thence across the Valdai Hills to tributaries of the Volga such as the Klyazma, the Oka, and the Moskva. Moscow was a transshipment point at which freight was directed to the tributaries of the Desna and the Dnieper rivers and thence south to the Black Sea.

Moscow became first a semi-independent principality and then the nucleus of a new Russian state. It was a long, hard process, marked by many setbacks and fierce fighting. Moscow had to beat back not only the Mongols but also invaders from the Baltic and Scandinavia. Little by little Moscow's power grew until finally under Ivan the Terrible the Russian state in the mid-1500's resumed a full-fledged role in European society.

The price Russia paid for two hundred years of subservience and rule of the Mongols was a terrible one. Even to this day it is still felt. At a time when Western Europe was being vitalized by the Renaissance, Russia still struggled with the darkness cast by Mongol domination. The development of arts and letters, science and industry in Russia lagged because of the terrible devastation—both material and human—wrought by the invaders.

The Mongols gave to Russian life and manners an admixture of Oriental ways that can, sometimes, be seen even today.

The Russian peasant, for instance, by tradition does not greet a superior by shaking hands or even bowing from the waist. He throws his hands over his head and brings them down in a full circle until they touch the ground. Or, a few years back, he might throw himself prostrate on the ground in a gesture of total submission. Ways of cunning and deceit were cultivated in Moscow in order to trick the oppressors. Some of the habits became permanent. We sometimes hear of a "Potemkin village"—a false front that the Russians put up to deceive a visitor. The name comes from a famous prime minister of Catherine II. When the Empress went on a visit to Southern Russia, Potemkin spent months in advance building a series of lavish and prosperous villages through which she could travel so that she would not learn the truth about the poverty of the country. Ambassadors in the time of Ivan the Terrible were customarily routed through specially beautified towns so they would form a false and exaggerated estimate of Russia's wealth. Visitors to Communist Russia are often taken on similar Potemkin tours so that they will carry back home inflated ideas of Soviet achievements.

From the Mongols, too, the Russians acquired the custom of plying their guests with strong drink. When guests were being entertained the gates to the palace were locked and bolted and no guest was permitted to leave until he became thoroughly intoxicated. The remnants of this habit can be seen today in the Russian insistence upon visitors' drinking toasts "*do dna*," or bottoms up, until their heads begin to whirl.

Without the unifying influence of the Russian Orthodox Church the survival of Russia under the Tatars would have been dubious. Christianity was brought in from Greece. There is a legend that the pagan prince Vladimir of Kiev adopted Greek Orthodoxy after first considering and rejecting the Jewish faith, the Moslem faith, and the Roman

Catholic Church. The legend is probably not true, but it is known that Vladimir became a convert to the Greek Orthodox faith in the year 989. He ordered all of the heathen idols that lined the banks of the Dnieper hurled into the river and he baptized his people, en masse, at the point of the sword. Some fled to the wilderness to escape, but Orthodox Christianity quickly became the general faith of Russia.

The Mongols were very liberal as far as religion was concerned. They actually did not interfere much in the internal affairs of their satrapies as long as tribute was promptly paid. Thus, despite the incursions of the Mongol hordes, the Orthodox Church was able to survive. It became a rallying point for Slav nationality.

At the time Russia adopted Orthodox faith the center of the church was Constantinople. But when the great Byzantine Empire fell to the Ottoman Turks, Russia became the Orthodox citadel. Ivan the Great deliberately sought to emphasize the role of Moscow as the heir to the glory of Constantinople. He took as his wife Zoë Palaeologue, princess of the Byzantine dynasty. Her uncle, the last Byzantine Emperor, died fighting the Turks on the walls of his city in 1453. Moscow then adopted Byzantium's double-headed eagle as its emblem. And the Great Elder of the Orthodox Church, Filofei of Pskov, wrote to the Grand

Prince Vasily III that "two Romes have fallen and the third stands while a fourth is not to be."

By this he meant that Rome itself, that is, the Roman Catholic Church, no longer was the true church; that the "second Rome," or Constantinople, had fallen to the Turks; and that the "third Rome," or Moscow, had inherited the spiritual and imperial leadership of the other two.

No wonder that the cathedral in Red Square, the church of St. Basil the Blessed, was for hundreds of years the center of special religious observances of deep Russian national significance.

The feeling that Moscow had a special mission to preserve and propagate the "true faith" of Orthodoxy throughout the world became a political and psychological phenomenon that deeply affected Moscow's life, particularly in the nineteenth century. To this day there are many who feel that much of the evangelizing drive of the Russian Communist movement sprang from this peculiar Russian sense of "mission" which stemmed from the role of the Orthodox Church.

When the Bolsheviks came to power in 1917, they brought to an end the use of St. Basil's and the Kremlin cathedrals for religious purposes. The Orthodox Church had been a bulwark of the Czarist regime and the Communists regarded it as a hated enemy. For some years St. Basil's was used as an antireligious museum, as was the great

Cathedral of Kazan in Leningrad. But in recent
years St. Basil's has been restored to its sixteenth-
century state. Its turrets and towers gleam with
gilt and many colors of paint. It is now preserved
as one of the precious historical monuments in
Russia.

The Communists have not ended their warfare
against religion. They carry on constant propa-
ganda against religious belief and sometimes taunt
and persecute priests and churchgoers. But services are permitted in about forty Orthodox
churches in Moscow, including the central Yelo-
khovsky Cathedral. There are also one small
Roman Catholic church, a large Jewish synagogue
and two small houses of prayer, one Moslem
mosque, a small Baptist church, and a few
churches of the Old Believers sect.

The Old Believers are a group of primitive
Orthodox faithful who broke about three hundred years ago with the main church over ques-
tions of minor changes in the wording of church
rituals. So fierce was the battle that at one time
the Old Believers locked themselves inside their
churches, set the churches ablaze and burned
themselves to death, singing religious chants,
rather than submit to any changes in the ritual.

This kind of faith borders on fanaticism. But
without it the Orthodox Church would hardly
have survived the years of Mongol occupation
and the ruthless opposition of the Soviet regime.

VIII. The Street of Saints and Barbarians

Toward the lower end of Red Square a narrow lane branches off to the east. It is one of the most ancient streets in Moscow. Once it was known as All Saints' Street and later on as the Street of the Barbarian. In recent times it has been called Stepan Razin Street after a peasant rebel leader who was executed in Red Square in 1671.

If we walk down Stepan Razin Street a block or two, making our way through the throngs hurrying to shop at the GUM department store, we come to a stout, squat house. It is built of stone with heavy windows, protected by ancient iron shutters. When the shutters are closed, the building, set back a bit from the street, looks like a small fortress. It is easy to see why it was known as the "Palace of the Siege." And it is not hard to believe that it held out successfully against lengthy Polish attack during the stormy Time of Troubles back in the early 1600's.

Today there is no plaque or mark on this house. Yet it possesses more than passing interest. This sturdy residence was the home of one of the great merchant families on which Moscow's rise to prominence was founded. The name of the family was Romanov. On February 13, 1613, the Council of Boyars, or Nobles, elected Michael Romanov, then a boy of seventeen, to the throne of Russia. Thus was founded the Russian dynasty that was to endure until it crashed in ruins in 1917.

It was no accident that the prince of a powerful merchant family was picked for the Russian throne. Trade had made Moscow great, and the Romanovs were among the greatest of the traders. Today the Romanov house is shut and a little dilapidated. For some years it was used as the Museum of Boyar Life. Then Stalin closed it and it has never been reopened. But it stands as a monument to the vigor of medieval Moscow. Just beside it rises a great construction site. Here Stalin planned to build a seventy-story Palace of Soviets. His successors canceled the plans and dismantled the steel work that already was going up. For years the site stood neglected, but now a big new hotel is planned here in what is called Zaryadye, the oldest settled part of Moscow, outside the Kremlin.

Archaeologists have found traces of a settlement in Zaryadye that goes back to the tenth or eleventh century. Here the barges brought grain on the Moskva River from Ryazan to feed the old city. There were nearby streets for trade in bread, meat, salt, and herring. Some of the old names survive. Criminals used to hide in the twisting streets of Zaryadye. Epidemics raged here. The terrible cholera epidemic of 1771, in which 40,000 of Moscow's 250,000 population lost their lives, is still remembered here. This plague, spread by the first Russo-Turkish War, gave impetus to the development of Russia's greatest "flea" market. This was located in Smolensk Square, where the towering building of the Soviet Foreign Office now stands. In the years after the Revolution the Smolensk market was a tragic sight. Here the "former people," as they were called, the men and women who had been supporters of the Czar or members of the nobility, stood, day after day, selling bits of jewelry, old medals, ancient fur pieces, portraits of their ancestors—anything to get a few rubles to enable them to buy bread. The market was abolished about the time of World War II.

In Moscow the saying is still to be heard: "The Smolensk market—son of cholera; the Sukharevsky market—daughter of war." Both actually existed at very early times, but Muscovites think of the Smolensk market as having been started by the cholera epidemic (the governor-general of the city issued an order that clothing of cholera victims could be sold only there) and of the Sukharevsky market as having had its start after the great fire of 1812, when so many Muscovites had to sell their half-burned possessions in order to survive.

Old Moscow, in fact, was a collection of great markets. Around the markets there frequently grew up colonies of thieves. Possibly the most notorious of these was the Khitrovka market, where in the days before the Revolution the police hardly dared enter. Here gathered escaped convicts from Siberia, exiles, beggars, robbers, criminals of all kinds.

Soviet authorities have steadily abolished the old Moscow markets. Nowadays persons who want to indulge in what is called "hand trading," that is, selling their clothing or personal possessions, must go to markets outside of Moscow in the suburbs. There are, however, thirty collective-farm or peasant markets in Moscow where farmers bring in their meat, vegetables, and fruits from nearby market gardens to sell to the city residents. These are one of the few vestiges of private enterprise that remain in Moscow. The farmers sell their eggs, butter, and sour cream for whatever prices the market will stand, and the proceeds go into their own pockets.

A PEASANT MARKET

One curious market is a survival of old Moscow days. This is the bird market near Taganka Square. Here on Sundays bird fanciers bring doves, pigeons, fighting cocks, finches, parrots, ducks, geese, and chickens for sale. They even bring puppy dogs and kittens. Thousands of people throng the market, particularly before "Bird Day." This is a Sunday in March traditionally dedicated to birds. For centuries it has been the custom in Russia to set birds free on that day. In the weeks just before Bird Day fathers and mothers throng the market to buy birds that their children can set free on the awaited day. The men in

THE BIRD MARKET

the market will sell a finch that is being freed for one ruble. If you are going to keep it in a cage, it costs three rubles. Just before Bird Day boys and men scour the nearby countryside, trapping thousands of birds that they bring into town, there to be sold and set free.

Few of those who buy and sell birds in Moscow on Bird Day have any knowledge of the origin of the curious custom. Actually it began in pagan times when among the primitive Slav tribes the coming of spring was symbolized by putting out the fires in the winter stoves and setting free the birds that had been kept in the hut through the winter's long months.

Somehow these ancient ceremonials became attached to Annunciation Day, which is celebrated by the Russian Orthodox Church on April 7, according to the Julian Calendar. This is March 25 by the Gregorian Calendar, used in Europe and the United States.

Orthodox believers say that they free birds on this day because Simeon and Anna brought presents of doves to the Mother of the Lord when she brought the Christ child to the temple. In many Orthodox churches there are ikons in which Simeon is represented holding the infant Christ while Anna presents a pair of doves.

This is a thoroughly confused fable. The Bible, in Luke 2, actually describes Mary and Joseph as bringing Jesus to the temple, where they offered the customary Hebrew sacrifice of two turtledoves to redeem their first-born. Simeon and Anna had been waiting at the temple to see the Christ child.

There is no connection, of course, between these events and the Annunciation of the Incarnation, made by the angel Gabriel to the Virgin Mary.

Not even Russian theologians have any idea how all the confusion arose, and, of course, the Soviet schools, which celebrate Bird Day on March 25, do not realize that the date is determined by one of the great events of the Christian Church.

In old Moscow, as in all old European cities, life was crowded together. The poor and the rich lived next door to each other. In one street were great riches. In the next incredible slums. A block or so from the Romanov house in Zaryadye was old Nikolskaya Street, which also led off Red Square. Today this is named October 25th Street in honor of the Bolshevik Revolution. The Bolshevik overturn occurred, according to the old Russian calendar, on October 25, 1917. That calendar lagged thirteen days behind the Gregorian calendar, which the rest of Europe followed. One of the first things Lenin did after getting into power was to put Russia on the Gregorian calendar. Thus, the Revolutionary anniversary was shifted from October 25 to November 7.

October 25th Street is sometimes called by Moscow residents the "Street of Enlightenment." Here the first Russian printing house, the Pechatny Dvor, was established by Ivan the Terrible in 1553. Here the first Russian book was printed, touching off such a storm from reactionary boyars and priests that the printers, Ivan Fedorov and his assistant, Peter Mstislavetz, had to flee to Lithuania. They were indicted on charges of witchcraft and threatened with burning at the stake.

On this street, too, the first Russian newspaper,

the *Vedomosti,* was issued in 1703 under Peter the Great. For generations the street was one of book-shops, particularly shops for rare books. Now most of Moscow's best bookstores are to be found on Kuznetsky Most (Blacksmiths' Bridge) and on Art Theater Street, near the Moscow Art Theater, possibly the most famous and best-known theater in the world. The Art Theater itself had its origin in a Nikolsky restaurant called the Slavyansky Bazaar. There on June 21, 1898, Konstantin S. Stanislavsky and V. I. Nemirovich-Danchenko

THE MOSCOW ART THEATER

met for dinner. Over a long meal and toasts of champagne the two men agreed to form the theater. Stanislavsky originated the realistic style of acting that is known in the United States as "the method." The Stanislavsky method may still be seen at the Art Theater, which faithfully preserves all of the traditions of its founders. The severely simple theater has as its symbol a stylized sea gull in memory of Anton Chekhov's play *The Sea Gull,* which was one of its first great artistic successes. Chekhov's plays still form a basic part of the Art Theater repertoire—*The Sea Gull, The Cherry Orchard, Uncle Vanya,* and *The Three Sisters.*

The Slavyansky Bazaar, where Stanislavsky and Nemirovich-Danchenko met, was often frequented by Chekhov as well. Here Chekhov and Leo Tolstoy once dined. The great Russian composers Tchaikovsky and Rimsky-Korsakov stayed at the Bazaar when they were in Moscow. The great singer Chaliapin dined there with Maxim Gorky. In restaurants like the Slavyansky Bazaar rich Moscow merchants loved to sit for hours, drinking boiling tea from glasses until perspiration rolled from their faces and they had to soak it up with big towels. But possibly the favorite amusement of pre-Revolutionary merchants and nobility was the gypsy restaurants where gypsy women, their gold coin necklaces and bracelets clicking, danced and sang songs of hopeless love like one called "Tzigansky Tabor," or the "Gypsy Camp." Rich men sometimes squandered their whole fortunes on gypsy entertainers. "Going to the gypsies" was a common thing in the late 1800's. The rich in Russia had a tradition of spending their money like water. They would go to a famous gypsy restaurant like the Yar, order the orchestra to play for them all night long, buy champagne and vodka by the barrel, and spend thousands of rubles in a single night. Such sprees might go on for weeks until the nobleman had spent all the wealth he possessed.

The Yar was the most famous of the gypsy restaurants. It still exists in Moscow, incorporated in the fine new Sovetskaya Hotel and serving as the hotel dining room. The décor has hardly changed since pre-Revolutionary days. Russians still love gypsy music. There is a gypsy theater in Moscow that puts on musical gypsy plays, and gypsy entertainers sometimes are to be found in the boat restaurants tied up along the Moskva River embankment.

But the Slavyansky Bazaar no longer exists. Its building has been used for a long time by the Moscow Puppet theater, the smaller of the two Moscow puppet establishments. The other puppet theater, that directed by Sergei Obratzov, is regarded by many as the best puppet theater in the world. The Slavyansky Bazaar building stands only a few doors from the site of the Pechatny Dvor. There now is to be found a beautiful Gothic building put up in 1814 after the great fire of 1812. It houses the Historical Archives Institute.

Moscow is built on a system of circular boulevards and radiating arterial streets that visitors sometimes compare with those of Paris. The comparison is apt. Just as in Paris the circular boulevards mark the rings of the walled or fortified Moscow of medieval times. The inner circle, of course, was that of the Kremlin walls itself. Beyond this was the "White Stone City," or "White City," as it was often called for short. This extended in the sixteenth century to a great brick wall in which there were a hundred and eight gates. The names of many of these gates persist as locality designations, but the gates themselves have long vanished. This became the "Boulevard Circle" when the wall was demolished. Here and there along the boulevard remnants of the old fortifications can still be seen. For most of its route this boulevard is pleasant, tree-shaded and passes through old and little-changed parts of Moscow.

One of the principal gates into the White City was located at what is now one of Moscow's busiest squares, Arbat Square, only a half-dozen blocks from the Kremlin. The square, the street running out of it, and the neighborhood called the Arbat got their name early in Moscow's history. It was called the *"orbat"* and was a camp or settlement for traders from the Arab or Oriental lands.

In the nineteenth century the Arbat quarter was one of the most stylish in Moscow. Here were the homes of the nobility and the wealthy. Today many of these great houses are embassies of foreign countries. Here on old Povarsky Street (the name comes from the word *povar,* meaning "cook," and the Czars' cooks once lived on this street) stands the great columned palace of the Dolgoruki family, descendents of the very Longarms who founded Moscow. This beautiful house is the original of the Rostov mansion, which is used by Tolstoy for the setting of his famous scenes in *War and Peace.* The house, little changed to this day, is occupied by the Union of Soviet Writers. The street is now called Ulitza Vorovsky and the house is No. 52.

Most of the great Russian writers and artists of the nineteenth century lived in this quarter of the city at one time or another. On a little back street called Sivtzev Vrazhek at No. 27 lived Alexander Hertzen when he wrote his famous book *"Who Are the Guilty?"* Alexander Pushkin, the greatest Russian poet, lived in a half-dozen locations in the Arbat, including houses on Gagarin Lane and on the Arbat itself. At No. 11 Kropotkin Street, in a beautiful Empire-style house, has been established the principal museum for the life and works of Leo Tolstoy. The street itself is named for Prince Kropotkin, a famous philosophical anarchist and revolutionary. At No. 2 Spiridonevsky Street Alexei Tolstoy, a relative of Count Leo Tolstoy and also a great Russian writer, lived at the time of his death in 1945. The street has been renamed for him and the house is a museum in his honor.

ALEXANDER PUSHKIN

During the Stalin days Arbat Street and Arbat Square thronged with plain-clothes men. The street is narrow and crowded. Stalin's limousine sped down it every day, traveling from his country house to the Kremlin. No one was permitted to live in any building along the Arbat without a special security clearance. Police would not permit pedestrians to cross the street or to stand for more than a moment or two. Sometimes it seemed that there were more police along the narrow route than there were ordinary civilians.

When Stalin's car appeared a special system of traffic lights flashed red all along the route and movement on cross streets was halted until his limousine had passed. The car always traveled at sixty miles an hour, preceded by one security car and followed by two more. The car Stalin rode in was a big old-fashioned Packard, specially made for him with bulletproof glass and an armored body.

After Stalin died all these elaborate security precautions were abandoned. Khrushchev and the other Soviet leaders began to ride around in ordinary cars. They even dispensed with the security tail car.

Arbat Square marked the limit of the White City. Beyond that, along Arbat Street and the present-day Arbat quarter, lay what was called the Zemlyanovo City—the City of Huts. Here in medieval times were settlements of bowmen, artisans, traders, and others who lived in what were called "brotherly courtyards," something like the guild groups of early London or Venice. This City of Huts extended to the present Garden Boulevard, which in the seventeenth century was marked by a wooden wall and a deep moat. When the wall came down, a pleasant boulevard with trees in the center and along the sides was built. However, in the 1930's Stalin had all the trees ripped out and turned the Garden Boulevard into a three-hundred-foot circumferential artery. This was done to facilitate the movement of troops and tanks around the city in case of an uprising. Now the Garden Boulevard is being transformed into a limited-access freeway to speed the movement of traffic in Moscow. Underpasses are being built for pedestrians. Pedestrian traffic is a special hazard in Moscow because many persons are peasants who are just in from the villages and who do not appreciate the dangers of fast-moving cars and trucks. Traffic underpasses are also being built at the principal intersections, such as Mayakovsky Square.

Beyond the Garden Boulevard wall, in the old days, there were other settlements of weaponers, farriers, coachmen, and workers of divers sorts.

One of the settlements was called the Nemetskaya, or German, settlement. The word *nemetskaya* means "the tongueless ones." In other words, those who didn't know Russian. Russians often applied the word to any foreigner. In this quarter all foreigners were forced to live. They were cut off from ordinary contact with Russians. Penalties for too close contact between foreigners and Russians were heavy. When the Danish ambassador under Ivan the Terrible married a Russian woman and asked for permission to take her back to Denmark, Ivan flew into a rage and threatened to chop off the ambassador's head.

Russian suspicion of foreigners was not born under the Bolshevik regime. It had been ingrained in the Russian character long before. Stalin's attitude resembled that of Ivan. He, like Ivan, applied strict restrictions on the contact between Soviet citizens and foreigners. He tried in every way to keep Russians from marrying foreigners. He forbade Russian wives of foreigners to leave the country, and even today Soviet authorities put every kind of obstacle in the path of "mixed" marriages.

The curious antagonism against Russian women's leaving Russia may stem to the days of the Tatar occupation. The Tatars used to ravage the countryside, rounding up Russian women

PETER THE GREAT

whom they shipped into slavery. They often raided Moscow and carried away women by the thousand. For two hundred years the slave markets of Asia and Turkey were thronged with Russian women and girls.

Old Moscow was the home of Russian conservatism. It was the center of the Slavophile movement. The supporters of this movement believed that Russia's future lay within herself. They strongly opposed the European leanings of Peter the Great which led him to found St. Petersburg and transfer the capital there from

Moscow. They opposed change. They strongly backed the Orthodox Church and its messianic tendencies. Peter fought these policies unceasingly. He imposed a tax on beards, which he felt symbolized old Russia's backwardness. His customs officials at the Moscow city gates were instructed to collect a ruble from any merchant or noble who wore a beard. For a peasant the fine was four kopeks.

Even in modern times the beard has been considered in Moscow to be a sign of backwardness. The Communist Party has tried to discourage the wearing of beards, particularly by young people. When young Russian beatniks began to appear on the streets, sporting beards like those their counterparts wore in Paris and New York, the Party workers called on them to shave their chins.

No problem over the centuries has concerned the rulers of Moscow more than that of backwardness. This was the driving force behind the reigns of Ivan the Great, Ivan the Terrible, Peter the Great, Catherine the Great, and, more recently Stalin.

Stalin, as terrible a dictator as the Russians ever endured, stated Russia's chronic problem in words as eloquent as it has ever inspired. Telling the Communist Party in 1931 why the pace of development must not slacken, he said:

"To slacken the pace would mean to lag behind; and those who lag behind are beaten. We do not want to be beaten. The history of old Russia was that she was ceaselessly beaten for her backwardness. She was beaten by the Mongol Khans. She was beaten by the Turkish Beys. She was beaten by the Swedish feudal lords. She was beaten by the Polish and Lithuanian Pans. She was beaten by the Anglo-French capitalists. She was beaten by the Japanese barons. She was beaten by all—for her backwardness. For military backwardness, for cultural backwardness, for political backwardness, for industrial backwardness, for agricultural backwardness. She was beaten because to beat her was profitable and went unpunished. Remember the words of the pre-revolutionary poet 'Thou art poor and thou art plentiful, thou art mighty and thou art helpless, Mother Russia.'"

To this day the rulers of Moscow continue to strive to overcome this backwardness.

IX. "ONLY GOD AND THE CZAR KNOW"

OVERLOOKING the great bend in the Moskva River there is a bluff from which you can see out over the whole of Moscow. Back in the 1890's this was a favorite spot for Sunday outings. Young men and young women, carrying accordions, guitars, and picnic lunches, used to gather on the open hillside. While some members of the party played songs, danced, and kept a sharp lookout for the police, the others would plot new revolutionary moves against the Czar's government.

In those days the bluffs were known as Sparrow Hills. Along the nearby Kaluga Road, Napoleon approached the city in 1812, and from these heights he watched Moscow burst into flames before his astonished eyes.

Today the view of the city is much changed. In the foreground where the Luzhniki swamps used to lie in the bend of the river now stands a 120,000-seat stadium and the huge Lenin Sports Palace. On the hills themselves arises the greatest ensemble of new buildings in Moscow. Dominating the group, which spreads across the plains toward the horizon, is the thirty-two-story central tower of the new scientific faculty of Moscow State University, which is the oldest in Russia. It was founded in 1755. For years it was housed in a cluster of ancient buildings on Mokhovaya Street, just a block from the Kremlin. Today the humanist faculties are still in the old quarter, grouped about a statue of Mikhail Lomonosov, the founder of Russian science.

On the Lenin Hills, as the bluff over the Moskva River is now known, has arisen a whole new university, dedicated to science. At a cost estimated at close to three-quarters of a billion dollars for buildings and equipment, the Soviet Government has erected one of the largest complexes of research institutes, laboratories, special schools for advanced studies, and technical facilities that exist anywhere in the world. Some eight thousand or nine thousand students are studying in the university itself, and thousands more are engaged in advanced research in affiliated laboratories and institutes. Among them are students from almost all the principal countries of the world. There are hundreds of students from each of the Communist countries. In recent years, under the exchange programs a number of Amer-

MOSCOW UNIVERSITY

ican, English, and French students have also been enrolled in Moscow University.

Just beyond the great university complex lies the Cheremushki Housing Development, the biggest new apartment project in Moscow. This is also one of the largest in the world. It is located in what used to be a little country village named Cheremushki, which means Wild Cherry. But there is not a trace of the village or the wild cherries left. All was obliterated by the bulldozers that cleared the land to permit the building of blocks of flats in which between 200,000 and 300,000 Moscovites have found new homes.

Americans often find the new Soviet construc-

BUILDING NEW FLATS

tion shoddy, and Russian builders admit that it could be vastly improved. But to the Muscovites who have moved into new flats after years of existence in "communal apartments"—old seven- and eight-room flats in which each family has but a room to itself and all share a common kitchen and bathroom—the defects of the new buildings seem minor.

South of the thirty-two-story university tower, according to the plans of the Moscow city architects, will be built a big new Palace of Soviets for government meetings. And a mile or two to the east it is proposed to erect a Pantheon in which will be placed to rest all the great figures of the Soviet Union.

Thus this enormous new Southwest Region of Moscow, as it is officially called, is being developed as the most imposing area of the city. It is crisscrossed by four- and six-lane boulevards. There are vast park areas, new complexes of shops which include Moscow's first self-service stores, new schools, new hospitals, new neighborhood clinics—"polyclinics," as they are called in Moscow—regional department stores, hotels, restaurants, and even a shop that, imposingly, is dedicated exclusively to the sale of radioactive isotopes.

This is the new Moscow—the Moscow of the post-Stalin era. It is linked to the older part of the city by fast autobus and trolley-bus service and by the rapidly expanding network of the Moscow Metro, the Soviet counterpart of the New York subway or the London Underground.

The Metro has long been considered by the Soviet regime as one of its brightest achievements. Construction was begun in 1931, and the first line, an eleven-mile segment, was opened in 1935. It now consists of nearly fifty miles of two-track lines. There are almost sixty stations and about 2,800,000 passengers daily. Many of the stations

A SUBWAY STATION

are so elaborately decorated with statuary, bas-reliefs, and ornamental columns that passengers have some trouble finding their way to and from the trains. They are built very deep in the ground, partly because of Moscow's swampy terrain and partly so the stations and tunnels can be used as air-raid shelters in case of need. During World War II, Stalin held a big Communist Party meeting in the Mayakovsky Metro Station while the Nazis were bombing Moscow. Once Stalin's picture and statue adorned most of the stations. But in 1962 the last Stalin mementos were obliterated.

Workmen even chiseled his face out of mosaic murals.

Many theories have been advanced as to why the Soviets spent so many hundreds of millions of rubles in marble, massive chandeliers, lavish fittings, carvings, and décor in their Metro system. One possible explanation is that the government could not afford to build housing, provide more food or better clothing at a time when it was investing so heavily in industrialization. So the beautiful Metro was built to give the workers a psychological lift. They had to live in slums, eat badly, and work until they were exhausted. But, morning and evening, they rode the Metro, which gave them a vision of what the Soviet system could achieve, once the country's economy had been built up.

INSIDE A SUBWAY
STATION

Just as the Metro was, in a sense, a symbol of the Soviet future in the 1930's, so the elaborately decorated thirty-two-story tower of the Moscow University was a symbol of the Soviet future of the 1950's.

From the very start of the Soviet regime education was given the highest priority. The illiteracy of Russia, the backwardness of the peasant, the ignorance epitomized by the old saying of the serfs that "I do not know—only God and the Czar know," the Slavic resignation to the fates—these were among the first targets of the new Communist regime.

A SUBWAY TRAIN

In 1917 Russia possessed far more people who did not know how to read and write than had mastered their letters. In Moscow two persons out of five were illiterate. Schooling was the exception, not the rule. Even a man like Premier Khrushchev had no formal schooling until four or five years after the Revolution, when the party sent him to classes for adults.

By the time the new Moscow University skyscraper was dedicated in 1953, the illiterate person was a rarity, particularly in Moscow. Even so the tower was intended to demonstate Soviet dedication to the twin principles of education and science—the principles that four years later enabled the Russians to send Sputnik aloft, followed by their astronauts Gagarin and Titov.

The best place for acquainting ourselves with the achievements of Soviet space technology is the rapidly expanding Exhibition of Industry and Agriculture, which occupies grounds of nearly six hundred acres on the northern city limits of Moscow, not far from Sokolniki Park, where the American Exhibition was held in 1959.

The Soviet Exhibition began before World War II as a kind of state fair. It was devoted to agricultural exhibits—prize cows, horses, and sheep. It had displays of grain, vegetables, and fruit from all over the Soviet Union.

It was closed during World War II and not reopened until 1954. Very quickly it was expanded into something like a permanent Soviet World Fair. Here is exhibited the model of the original Soviet earth satellite. Here are capsules such as Gagarin and Titov occupied. Here is a working model of an atomic pile, showing how the automatic controls enable a technician to manipulate it from a distance. Here are models of the new oxygen-process Soviet steel mills, automated coal mines, new Siberian hydroelectric installations that will generate up to four million kilowatts of power—twice as much as any plant in the U.S.A. —and outlines of the Soviet program to put the first man on the moon.

There is a hall filled with every kind of Soviet tractor, combine, agricultural machine, and earth-moving device. There is a display of Soviet trucks and automobiles, all looking very much like their American counterparts.

There are elaborate fountains, a dozen different kinds of restaurants, lakes with swans and flamingos. Nowhere in the Soviet Union can you more quickly get an idea of the diversity of peoples, the multitude of nationalities, the variation in climate, soils, and terrain than in this exhibit. Each of the big nationalities—the Ukrainians, the Byelorussians, the Uzbeks, the Turkmans, the Georgians and the Kazakhs—has a pavilion decorated in national style, attended by nationals in their colorful dress, demonstrating the products peculiar to their region.

Almost every visitor to Moscow, whether from the provinces of Russia or some foreign land, comes to the exhibition. It is like a short course in Soviet plans and intentions, a forecast of the kind of technology and the nature of life which the Soviet rulers hope to create for the people of Moscow and all of the U.S.S.R. as years go on and they come closer to their goal of Communism. For, while we think of the Soviet system as "Communist," the Soviets themselves describe it as "Socialist." Communism, they say, will come only after, perhaps, twenty or twenty-five years of hard, hard work. They define Communism as a system of "From each according to his abilities; to each according to his needs." The present system is said to be one of "From each according to his abilities; to each in accordance with his work." One of the central exhibits at the permanent Moscow Exhibition depicts the Khrushchev blueprint for achieving Communism. This was adopted by the Twenty-Second Congress of the Communist Party at their session in the new Kremlin Palace of Soviets, held in October 1961.

Moscow citizens are proud of their city. They

are proud of its long and troubled past. They are proud of its present. They enjoy showing visitors about their great museums—the Lenin Museum, which is dedicated to the life of the founder of the Revolution (and also contains a display of the achievements of Premier Khrushchev); the State Historical Museum and the Museum of the Revolution, which detail the rise of the Bolshevik Party and the overthrow of the Czarist regime; the Moscow Museum of Planning and Reconstruction, where the city's past—and future—are on display. They glory in the art treasures of the Tretyakov Gallery, with its collection of ancient ikons by Rublov, its masterworks by classic Russian painters such as Repin, Shishkin, and Suri-

LENIN LIBRARY

PREMIER KHRUSHCHEV

kov, its reserve collection of modernistic Russian painters like Chagall, Malevich and Kandinsky. They are equally proud of the Pushkin Gallery, which is dedicated to classical Western art and includes one of the finest European collections of modern French painters—Picasso, Manet, Monet, Renoir, Matisse, Gauguin, and Van Gogh. These works are part of a collection assembled by two wealthy Moscow collectors, Morozov and Shchukin, just before World War I. For years the magnificent paintings were kept under lock and key because Stalin regarded modern painting as decadent. Only after his death was the collection divided into two parts, one for the famous Hermitage Gallery in Leningrad and the other for the Pushkin Museum, and presented once again to public view.

The greatest library in Moscow is named for Lenin. Like the Moscow collection of French impressionist paintings, its basic fund of books originally was privately owned—the great library of Count Nikolai Rumyantzev, which numbered 28,500 volumes. Now, however, the Lenin Library is the second largest in the world, numbering more than 20,000,000 items, including about 9,000,000 books. Only the Library of Congress in Washington is larger.

Moscow has twenty-nine theaters, topped by the world-famous Bolshoi with its ballet and opera company, the historic Maly, famous for traditional Russian plays by Ostrovsky, the Art Theater, and the Vakhtangov Theater. The Mayakovsky Theater, the Satire Theater, and the new Contemporary Theater present experimental plays that are beginning to break with the drab conformity imposed on the stage by Stalin's dictatorial taste. There are two beautiful concert halls, a half-dozen dance ensembles, including the Moiseyev group, which has scored brilliant successes in the United States, and the Moscow State Circus,

where clowns and dancing bears, trained horses
and high-wire artists perform in a permanent am-
phitheater the year round. And there's an animal
theater, called Durov's Corner, where American
possums, black-and-gray magpies, cats and squir-
rels put on a show, trained according to the principles of the Durov family—in which only
kindness and rewards, never punishment, are permitted.

This is the Moscow of culture and art and
science and education of which every Muscovite
is proud. These are the fine elements in the Russian capital city of which its citizens boast. They
have come, they feel, a long way from the day
when their great compatriot Hertzen could write
just a century ago that Moscow was merely an
overgrown, rich Russian village. "At each step,"
said Hertzen, "you are reminded of the isolated
Slavonic oriental way of life. The Muscovite
citizen has no aim at all. He is generally satisfied
with himself." That was a Moscow where not a
few burghers still lived by the ancient Domovoy,
or Householder's Rules, that described how the
master should beat his wife and children in the
most "sensible, painful, frightening and profitable
manner." And warned of the house spirits, which
lived behind the great brick stoves, and the *leski,*

or forest spirits that were apt as not to carry off young girls while they were out picking mushrooms.

Today's Moscow laughs at such old wives' talk. It is a boisterous, bustling city, growing fast, filled with young people and new people from the provinces, hurrying to get ahead, jostling each other in the stores, on the sidewalks, and at the big soccer games in Dynamo Stadium, not as well mannered as it might be but generally hospitable to strangers in rough-and-ready fashion. It's a city on the move, working hard in its thousand plants and factories, thronging to the beaches on the Moskva River in the summertime and to the skating rinks in Gorky Park in winter, tearing down old buildings and throwing up new ones. It is a city that has seen great tragedy under both the Czars and the Communists. It has survived many an ordeal in its more than eight hundred years and would not be surprised if more ordeals lay ahead.

But it is an ambitious city, too. The plans for its future are grandiose. "Come back in ten years," a Muscovite tells you. "You won't recognize the place." If the past few decades of Moscow history are any guide to the future, the Muscovite's sweeping promise may bear fruit.

INDEX